Adderley Primary School, Sa   34
                                               35
Rizwana Begum (9)   ~~pnia Morgan (7)   36
Luqman Guled Mohamed (10)   —   Annabelle Holmes (7)   37
Amelia Islam (10)   3   Buddy Addis (7)   38
Hooriya Arif (11)   4   Darcy Gorwood (7)   39
Joumana Itouni (10)   6   Harvey Martin (7)   40
Abdul Abraar (10)   8   Elsa Snowball (7)   41
Bibi Kalsoom (10)   9   Isla McQuillan (7)   42
Aqsa Afzal (10)   10   Jatou Cham (7)   43
Sana Malik (10)   11   Imogen Craven (8)   44
Bashir Ali (10)   12   Chloe Hodson (7)   45
Aleena Hussain (9)   13   Maddy Hewitt (9)   46
                                    Leo March (8)   47
Chatsworth Primary School,   Ted Stenson (7)   48
Hounslow   Joey Butterworth (7)   49
                                    Thomas Swindles (7)   50
Jace De Souza (7)   14   Marta Kennedy (7)   51
Daro Shalli (11)   16   Ruby Slater (8)   52
Ononna Kabir (10)   17   Freddie Watson (8)   53
Bella Ramos (8)   18   Pixie Freer (7)   54
Vinisha Pandya (9)   19   Oscar Haslam (9)   55
Dariia Kurylyk (9)   20   Max Kirby (8)   56
                                    Bethany Littler (7)   57
Dringhouses Primary School, York Roddy Gavin (8)   58
                                    Edie Marchant (8)   59
Florence Aldridge (8)   21   Owen Evans (7)   60
Isla McIntyre (7)   22   Noah Gibson (7)   61
Oliver Cawdell (8)   24
Amara Crampton (9)   25   **Kobi Nazrul Primary School,**
Eloise Hanson (8)   26   **Whitechapel**
Ziva Shah-Martin (7)   28
James Goforth (8)   30   Radiyah Ahmed (9)   62
Noah Wordsworth (8)   31   Khadijah Siddique (7)   64
Savannah Limbert (7)   32   Yunus Uddin (7)   65
Addison Davies (7)   33   Fariha Sayed (10)   66

First published in Great Britain in 2022 by:

YoungWriters® Est. 1991

Young Writers
Remus House
Coltsfoot Drive
Peterborough
PE2 9BF
Telephone: 01733 890066
Website: www.youngwriters.co.uk

All Rights Reserved
Book Design by Ashley Janson
© Copyright Contributors 2021
Softback ISBN 978-1-80015-808-5

Printed and bound in the UK by BookPrintingUK
Website: www.bookprintinguk.com
YB0496F

FOREWORD

For Young Writers' latest competition This Is Me, we asked primary school pupils to look inside themselves, to think about what makes them unique, and then write a poem about it! They rose to the challenge magnificently and the result is this fantastic collection of poems in a variety of poetic styles.

Here at Young Writers our aim is to encourage creativity in children and to inspire a love of the written word, so it's great to get such an amazing response, with some absolutely fantastic poems. It's important for children to focus on and celebrate themselves and this competition allowed them to write freely and honestly, celebrating what makes them great, expressing their hopes and fears, or simply writing about their favourite things. This Is Me gave them the power of words. The result is a collection of inspirational and moving poems that also showcase their creativity and writing ability.

I'd like to congratulate all the young poets in this anthology, I hope this inspires them to continue with their creative writing.

Nura Ali (10)	67
Ismaaeel Choudhury (7)	68
Ameera Islam (10)	69
Khadijah Hoque (9)	70
Amirah Azim (7)	71
Iffat-Anisha Fazlul Haque Yeasmin (8)	72
Maisha Ali (7)	73
Sulaiman Ahmed (7)	74
Ryan Kai (9)	75
Arshi Islam (7)	76
Mikaeel Karim (7)	77
Chad Hossin (8)	78

Ponteland Primary School, Ponteland

Molly Fielding	79
Takara Barton (7)	80

St Margaret's CE School, Rottingdean

Dolly Griffiths (10)	81
Isabella Dye (10)	82
Lily McCaw (10)	83
Jacob Lord (10)	84
Evie Dearnley (10)	86
Albert Luis Stevenson (10)	88
Harley Knight (10)	89
Astrid Dickie (10)	90
Albie Knight (10)	91
Danielle Fadario (10)	92
Luke Simmons (10)	93
Pippa Payne (11)	94
Teddy Griffiths (11)	95
Ellison Sedge (11)	96
Jack Rowden (10)	97
Havannah Ballard (10)	98
Maya Marco (10)	99
Ying Toong (10)	100

Stanhope Primary School, Greenford

Lydia Lima Soares Dos Santos (10)	101
Franki Raczynski (11)	102
Anoja Nadarasa (11)	104
Amina Baahmed (8)	105
Dunmolaoluwa Hannah Ojo (10)	106
Shruthi Sellathamby (10)	107
Kaiden Watson (8)	108
Anwar Dardak (7)	109
Araani Sivasubramaniam (8)	110
Charlize Erese (11)	111
Harper Nolan (8)	112
Sean Butt (10)	113
Sana Hashimi (10)	114
Dipanshu Shah (7)	115
Zara Hussein (7)	116
Armin Saberipour (7)	117
Dorcas Nsubuga (11)	118
Marwan Sidani (10)	119
Camiyah Tuahene Richards (7)	120
Tnishpreet Kaur (7)	121
Riaz Mahabir (11)	122
Anmol Singh (7)	123
Corey Watson (7)	124
Sana Usman (10)	125
Nesha Angelova (9)	126
Ellia Demiri (8)	127
Zayan Hamid (7)	128
Gulled Talyanle (11)	129
Shalini Aruchuna (8)	130
Odai Alarabi (7)	131
Zain Adeen (7)	132
Sofia Wozniak (7)	133

THE POEMS

This Is Me

I'm as funny as a clown,
If you ever feel down
I will turn you the other way round.
I'm kind because whenever I meet someone new
I have a smile on my face.
It's always fun to make a new mate.
I am gentle and light as a feather.
I'm as bright and open like the sunny weather.
Sometimes I can feel nervous and anxious but I never let my feelings take
The best of me,
I'm strong and I can do anything I put my mind up to, you see.
I like to make new friends and meet new people,
You can describe me as funny, generous, fearless
Brave and determined.
I'm good at art, sports, and acting.
Before I end my poem in the future
I aspire to become a doctor because I want to help people, you know it.

Rizwana Begum (9)
Adderley Primary School, Saltley

My Lovely Bed

I lie on my bed
My lovely bed
The bed that makes me dream of poetry so high, it's precious.
I sleep to dream of adventurous getaways and dreamy words,
I can't express
In the rose of the morning light, I find myself fixed flat on the floor
I look above my bed but find it difficult to leave your sight
My lovely bed, please stop mourning
I promise you of stories that will last until the following morning
Every morning I make my bed
And on my arrival, I feel like a guest
My lovely bed treats me good, as you have done for years
You have witnessed my ups and downs when I'm ill or feel sad
You know how to treat a lonely teardrop
So tuck me in my lovely bed, I hope to meet you in the night.

Luqman Guled Mohamed (10)
Adderley Primary School, Saltley

The Snowman And The Hungry Bunny

A little snowman had a long orange nose,
Then along came the bunny and what do you suppose?
That hungry little bunny looking for some dinner,
Jumped as high as it can go and grabbed that carrot nose,
The bunny slowly going still hungry and wanted more,
"Stop! Stop! Stop!" the snowman said.
"Where are you going on such a windy day?"
"Looking for food," the bunny said with a smile on his face.
The snowman shouted, "There!"
A field full of food for the bunny and a new nose for the snowman
And they waddled away into the deep snow.

Amelia Islam (10)
Adderley Primary School, Saltley

A Positive Mindset Of A Wonderful Person

A wonderful person I am
Reading and writing
Playing and hopping
Always more to do!

A wonderful person I am
Generous and humble
Always respectful!

A wonderful person I am
A heart full of courage
With a spoonful of self-belief
Always open to new ideas!

A wonderful person I am
Thinking outside the box
Always respecting people's views!

A wonderful person I am
Wondering around

But not in a square
Always creative!

A wonderful person I am
Religious, friendly and
Very caring too!

Wonderful people we all are!
As we are all equal!
All unique!

Let's be thankful to God too!

Hooriya Arif (11)
Adderley Primary School, Saltley

Poetry

Poetry is inside me,
Believe me, it's not hard,
All you need is to be
Confident you can write poetry!

I love poetry,
I have inspiration inside me,
Giving me lovely words,
To make me write poetry!

It can be about anything,
A talent, food or favourite thing,
Believe me, you just write and...
Magically it's words of poetry!

It doesn't have to rhyme,
All you need is passion and self-belief,
A splash of commitment and
The poem is ready!

Inspiration is always knocking on the door,
Whispering to me ideas,
Even when I'm asleep,
Without it, I can't write poetry.

Joumana Itouni (10)
Adderley Primary School, Saltley

Books! Books!

I feel there's just one song to sing
And that's a song of books!
I can't think of another thing
Except them and their looks,
All your companies, these black soldiers,
Never left my side, summer evenings, winter dawns
With me they did abide.

Books! Books! Right and left!
Knowledge by the yard.
Books! Books! Build and heft,
And problems daunting hard.
Books with dates and books with songs.
And books that make you cry,
Books that like great city throng
Went we singing by.

Awake it's a world of books!

Abdul Abraar (10)
Adderley Primary School, Saltley

Happiness

Adderley Primary School is the greatest school
With wonderful teachers and amazing food
It taught me to be brave and strong and independent.
My aspiration is to be a doctor
And save lives and deaths.
My favourite thing about me is I am polite
And right I am
Strong as a boxer
And I want to encourage a youngster
That they can achieve anything they want in life.
Life is alright and it is right
Nothing can stop you so go
Out there have your life and time
And spend it on something nice
I hope you listened to my poem, please pick me.

Bibi Kalsoom (10)
Adderley Primary School, Saltley

Dynamite

My name is Aqsa,
I love food, my favourite food is pizza and chips,
On top of that it is apple juice no
It's Coca-Cola.
I like dancing but it isn't poetry
"Poetry"
I think of poetry every two or three seconds in my mind of creation.
I go outside and every time my thoughts come back to me one or two times.
In my mind, it all stops to me all my thoughts it might go away from me.
I have three siblings,
Including me, it is all difficult listening to my brother
Chatting all day, all night for me to see.

Aqsa Afzal (10)
Adderley Primary School, Saltley

Unique

This is me, no one else can be way up high in my dreams you'll see,
Far away in a town so small, everyone here is oh so tall.
Look at me, tell me what you see.
Some might say I'm not as you seem,
In the trees, so alone and discreet,
Let me tell you I'm incomplete.
All the others don't give me any bother,
All because I have an odd feather,
But don't feel bad; I like to be alone,
Then that way I'm always unknown.
What you see is a bird so unique,
We finally realise it's not me who was weak.

Sana Malik (10)
Adderley Primary School, Saltley

Cycles

As the days go by,
And as the wind roams in the wild.
As the seasons change,
From autumn to winter,
Winter to spring,
Spring to summer,
As the cycle repeats itself again,
The tree cycle does too,
The fruits seed and leaves fall when it reaches autumn,
And they all go back into the ground,
Until they turn into plants then into trees,
As the cycle repeats itself again.

Bashir Ali (10)
Adderley Primary School, Saltley

Oh, How I Love Nature

Oh, how I love nature!
I go bike riding every day,
As if I was part of nature
The birds are tweeting as the sun shines bright
Like a shooting star from outer space.
The green, gorgeous leaves falling from the wise old willow tree.
The sky turns baby pink, as the butterflies
Flutter over the pretty pink roses.

Aleena Hussain (9)
Adderley Primary School, Saltley

All About Me

This is a poem that's about me.
From the top of my head to the soles of my feet.
I'm funny, I'm happy.
I'm helpful,
I'm kind,
I've no favourite colour,
I can't make up my mind.

I really love school,
My teachers,
My friends.
I love reading books right up to the end.
I'm sporty,
I'm friendly,
I'm cheerful,
I'm glad,
I love making maps in my great big art pad.

I'd eat pizza all day,
I just couldn't stop or
Juicy strawberries with ice cream on top.

I'm jolly,
I'm silly,
I'm funny,
I'm wise,
I love eating cheeseburgers and curly French fries.

Jace De Souza (7)
Chatsworth Primary School, Hounslow

This Is Me

I like to play basketball,
I am decently tall,
I sigh when I fall,
I love to go to the lunch hall,
And once I ran into a wall.

I also like to play table tennis,
But when it rains I hear *splat, splat*.
Then I run home and I groan and moan,
Then I watch TV but never with my top hat.
And I eat my KitKat.

The only way I am considered bad,
Is when I call people mad
I like percentages and angles but I don't like to add
When I start my homework I am definitely sad.

I like to play video games after tea,
So please don't judge,
As this is me.

Daro Shalli (11)
Chatsworth Primary School, Hounslow

This Is Me

Bright and comfy
I really like lemon tea
My favourite animal are parrots
I don't really like carrots.

I actually like netball
And I really like fall
History makes me moan
Whereas art makes me have a happy tone.

I'm quiet, I'm shy
But what makes me happy is apple pie.

Most of my days aren't that bad
I have a brother that almost never gets mad
I don't like fizzy drinks
My favourite colour isn't pink.

And that is a rap all about me!

Ononna Kabir (10)
Chatsworth Primary School, Hounslow

Me, Myself And I

I run as fast as a cheetah.
I paint like actual artists.
I play basketball like a pro.
I dance on the stage while the audience says "Woah!"
I am as kind as a nurse.
I am funny, smart and quiet like a mouse.
I discover the world by a step like a hunter.
I'm adventurous.
My hair is the midnight sky.
I'm a ballerina, I twirl like a tornado.
I'm a tap dance, I tap to the beat.
This is me.

Bella Ramos (8)
Chatsworth Primary School, Hounslow

Me

I am an ice cream licker - lick
I am a Diwali celebrater - spark
I am a happy kangaroo - leap
I am a pretty angel - flutter
I am a reading bookworm - wiggle
I am an art superstar - splash
I am a birthday lover - pop
I am a clown cheerer - clap
I am a dog petter - stroke
I am an ice lolly gobbler - gobble
I am a kind friend - laugh.

...This is me...

Vinisha Pandya (9)
Chatsworth Primary School, Hounslow

This Is Me

I'm a lover of small animals.
I'm a drawing master.
I'm a singing star.
I'm an ice cream lover.
I'm fantastic at the piano.
My eyes are like chocolate cake.

   S inging is my favourite job.
   T eamwork is my best.
   A lisa is my favourite name.
   R eading is most interesting for me.

Dariia Kurylyk (9)
Chatsworth Primary School, Hounslow

A Recipe Poem All About Marvellous Magical Me

To conjure me you will need the following things:
58g of some musical, special instrument.
78ml of Dringhouses Primary School.
79ml of cute cats.
1 gallon of flabbergasting friends.
15lb of a caring family.
10lb of stunning homemade pizza.
8 birthdays.
50g of Liverpool.

The way to create me is to follow these steps:
First of all, you need to grab the 79g of cute cats.
58g of musical, magical instruments and
50g of Liverpool add them in.
Next, stir it up nice and carefully.
With care add the 78ml of Dringhouses Primary School.
1 gallon of friends and
Caring family.
Pour it onto baking paper.

Florence Aldridge (8)
Dringhouses Primary School, York

How To Build Amazing Me

To construct me you will need the following ingredients:
An animal and insect filled bedroom,
10lb adventure and singing,
1 spoonful of biking,
5lb of shyness,
50ml of fun,
A pinch of happiness,
A dollop of friendliness,
A dollop of silliness,
4lb sense of humour.

To make me you need to do the following:
First, add the 4lb sense of humour,
Then, pour in an insect and animal-filled bedroom,
Next, slowly blend in 10lb adventure and singing with a spoonful of biking,
Later, chop up 5lb of shyness,
After, that add in 50ml of fun,
Next, add a pinch of happiness,
After that, add in a dollop of friendliness,

Finally, add in a dollop of silliness,
And cook until glazed.
This is me.

Isla McIntyre (7)
Dringhouses Primary School, York

How To Create Amazing Me

The following items will be needed:
A large leather pumped-up football.
100ml of fizzy drinks and three doughnuts!
An acoustic and electric guitar.
A smart mind.
50g of honesty.

Follow these steps to make me:
First, add 100ml of fizzy drinks, Sprite worked best, into a large pan.
After, add the leather pumped-up football in with the fizzy drinks.
Now put the doughnuts in one by one.
Next, thoroughly chop the electric and acoustic guitars and then slowly add them in.
Now, pour in 50g of honesty and stir steadily.
Finally, blend the smart mind and gently spread over the top of the pan.
This is me.

Oliver Cawdell (8)
Dringhouses Primary School, York

How To Create Funny Fabulous Me!

To construct me, you will need these ingredients:
A football-filled mind.
A random splash of friends.
A huge drop of fun.
A bunch of chicken nuggets.
A dash of Roblox.
Next, a lot of beds and sleep.
Lastly, you add a sprinkle of mischief.

A recipe poem to create me:
Firstly add a football-filled mind.
A random splash of friends.
A huge drop of fun.
Next, you will need to add a bunch of chicken nuggets.
Stir in a dash of bed and sleep.
Lastly, add in a sprinkle of mischief.
Then mix it all together and *boom* you made me.

Amara Crampton (9)
Dringhouses Primary School, York

How To Create The Amazing Mindblowing Me!

To make me you will need the following ingredients:
A music mind brother.
A lifetime of hot, fresh pizza.
An electronics-filled bedroom.
Five buckets of movies and popcorn.
A cup of funny friends.
Crazy dogs.

To build me you will need the following instructions:
First of all, pour five buckets of movies and popcorn!
After that slowly add in the lifetime of hot, fresh pizza.
Stir gently while mixing in the crazy dogs.
After stirring, spread the electronics-filled bedroom.

Finally, plop on the cup of friends.

That is how to make the amazing me!

Eloise Hanson (8)
Dringhouses Primary School, York

How To Make The Nice Kind Me

To create the happy me, you will need the following things:
A sprinkle of shine.
A sprinkle of sprinkles.
A teaspoon of nature.
A handful of music.
A dollop of sisters.
A dollop of gymnastics.
A dash of fun.
A dollop of cats and puppies.

Firstly, drop a dollop of gymnastics,
Next, sprinkle shine,
Then sprinkle sprinkles,
After put a dash of fun,
After that put a dollop of sisters,
Then mix harshly.
Next, put a dollop of puppies and cats.

After put a teaspoon of nature,
After that stir and put a handful of music.
This is me.

Ziva Shah-Martin (7)
Dringhouses Primary School, York

How To Construct Amazing Me

These are my ingredients:
1 teaspoon of fangs,
A pinch of fun,
A dollop of mint,
A drop of blood,
A sprinkle of speed,
A bar of chocolate,
A dash of brightness.

To make me, you will need to do this:
Firstly, add a drop of blood.
Next, put a dash of brightness until a beam of light shoots out.
Then stir the speed to make it cook fast.
After that chop up the chocolate bar into small pieces and drop them in while adding the mint.
A few minutes later add the brightness.
Finally, add the fangs with a pinch of fun.
This is me.

James Goforth (8)
Dringhouses Primary School, York

How To Construct Marvellous Me!

To construct me you will need the following items:
A music-mad mind.
A sprinkle of sport.
A generous dollop of nature.
100g of biking.
An adventurous, exciting comic.
A bowl of warm tomato soup.

You will need to do the following things:
First of all, gently add 100g of biking.
Then spread on a sprinkle of sport.
Next, gently pour in a bowl of warm tomato soup.
After that, stir in a dollop of nature.
A few minutes later delicately mix in adventurous, exciting comics.
Finally, add in a music-mad mind.

Noah Wordsworth (8)
Dringhouses Primary School, York

How To Make The Kind Helpful Me

To create me you will need the following ingredients:
A glistening magic chime to bring love.
A generous handful of unicorn magic.
1 Pokéball.
A pinch of science.
10 grams of art.
3ml of karate.

To make me you will need to do the following things:
First, shred the chime into the bowl.
Carefully sprinkle in the unicorn magic.
Roll the Pokéball in the mixture.
After that add in a pinch of science.
Now pour in the 10 grams of art.
Last but not least add 3ml of karate.

Savannah Limbert (7)
Dringhouses Primary School, York

How To Make Marvellous Me

To create me you will need these things:
A dollop of ice cream,
A drop of yoghurt,
An endless supply of books,
A pinch of laughter,
One teaspoon of melted chocolate,
A book-filled bedroom.

To make me you will need to do this:
Firstly, put in a pinch of laughter.
Then add a book-filled bedroom.
Add one teaspoon of melted chocolate.
After that pour in a dollop of ice cream and a drop of yoghurt.
Finally, add an endless supply of books.

Addison Davies (7)
Dringhouses Primary School, York

How To Make Me

To construct me, you will need:
A dollop of kindness and mischief.
A generous handful of friends.
A sprinkle of daredevils
A big dollop of football.

To make me:
First, you will need to add ice-cold water.
Secondly a big dollop of football.
A few minutes later put lime colour and a sprinkle daredevils
Then a dollop of kindness and mischief.
Finally, simmer a generous handful of friends.
Stir slowly and roughly in the cauldron.

Abigail Laing (8)
Dringhouses Primary School, York

Paige Torbet

P aige, that's me. I love puppies.
A nimals are my favourite thing.
I 'm an animal lover.
G irls rule the world!
E mma is the name of my mum.

T igers are my favourite animal.
O n TV my favourite program is powerful Pokémon.
R eading books about animals is fun.
B lackberries are my favourite berry.
E ating fish and chips is the best meal.
T his is me.

Paige Torbet (7)
Dringhouses Primary School, York

All About Me

I am a football superstar,
My eyes are blue marbles,
My hair is as soft as a panda cub,
I am a burger burglar,
My pet fish Finely is as scaly as a
Rolled up armadillo,
You will see me riding my bike in a blink of an eye,
I am as jumpy as a kangaroo,
I am as fast as a cheetah,
I gobble down fruit like a munching monster,
I am as cheeky as a monkey.
I've got a secret that nobody knows
This is me.

Sophia Morgan (7)
Dringhouses Primary School, York

All About Myself

I have a dog called Ronnie he is a black Labrador.
I have a brother called George,
Sometimes he is angry or happy and he likes dinosaurs and cars.
I am great at gymnastics, I like the bars.
My eyes are blue as bluebells,
My hair is blondish-brown like sand.
I am a great friend.
My friend is Pixie.
I am arty and messy, I love painting,
I have lost five teeth.
I am kind.
This is me.

Annabelle Holmes (7)
Dringhouses Primary School, York

How To Make Marvellous Me

To create me you will need:
A meerkat-filled bedroom
An Unspeakable hat
A cheesy pizza with a stuffed crust
A cat's tail
A sofa
A rabbit called Benjy.

Firstly put the cat's tail in the circle.
Then put the pizza in the ring.
Then mix it up slowly and put it in the pan and stir fast.
Then add the meerkat bedroom.
Finally, squeeze in the sofa.

Buddy Addis (7)
Dringhouses Primary School, York

The Dainty Dancing Darcy Dolphin

You will need;
A pot of golden paint
A shelf of storybooks
A squirrel's clicks
A jar of fun
And some love and mischief.

Take the jar of fun and pour it in.
Then put in the squirrel's clicks
And the pot of golden yellow paint.
Take the love and mischief and shelf of storybooks
And then cook until golden, long and fair.

This makes me!

Darcy Gorwood (7)
Dringhouses Primary School, York

How To Build The Wonderful Me

You will need a bedroom full of football posters.
Pour in a hug and bowl of hot chips.
You will need a drop of fun and a bit of mischief.
A lot of burgers.
You will need a football mind.
You will need a lot of chips and crisps and burgers.

Firstly, add in a drop of fun and a bit of mischief.
100kg of kindness.
A generous handful of football.
A lot of sugar.

Harvey Martin (7)
Dringhouses Primary School, York

About My Wonderful Personality

I am a mega cool dancer, lots of styles,
I am a super learner,
I am a lover of chapter books and reading,
Jacqueline Wilson is my favourite,
I am generous, caring and arty,
I have two pets, a hamster and a rabbit,
My pets always cheer me up when I am feeling blue,
I am really energetic,
My hair is as silky as cotton,
My eyes are bluey-green,
This is me.

Elsa Snowball (7)
Dringhouses Primary School, York

Glowing Disco

I love books.
I am a cat lover.
I am a pizza thief,
I love swimming
And I love singing,
From imaginative,
I am never as sad as a droopy bluebell.
I am always as happy as a sunflower.
I am a crazy girl,
I love to rock,
My cat is as cute as a mini teddy because he is so fluffy!
I light up the night on the disco floor!
This is me.

Isla McQuillan (7)
Dringhouses Primary School, York

The Incredible Me

To make this outstanding recipe you will need the following things:
A collection of Daredevil posters.
15ml of fresh and smooth orange juice.
10 boxes of pizza.
20 bags of popcorn.
A Descendants CD.
A bowl.
A knife.

To make me:
First, get a knife, chop the pizza and put it in the oven.
Then find the bowl and stir the orange juice.

Jatou Cham (7)
Dringhouses Primary School, York

This Is Me

I'm a superstar swimmer when I jump in a pool,
I hop and I jump and spring from the ground,
Though eight-legged creatures make me scream and cower,
But my parents say I stream with power.
I spend my time at school with my lunatic friends,
At home, I am an artist and an author with my fancy pens.
My head is full of creative colour,
This is me.

Imogen Craven (8)
Dringhouses Primary School, York

What I'm Like

I am a crazy person
An animal lover.
I'm good at making people laugh,
I'm a blast at swimming,
I'm good at English.
I love rainbows,
I'm the disco of the night,
I love pandas.
I hate spiders,
My favourite colour is black as the night sky,
My dream is powers.
I love going to the park
This is me.

Chloe Hodson (7)
Dringhouses Primary School, York

Welcome To My World

I am a flexible mover dancing my dreams,
I am a fan of listening to music,
I am a lover of games Roblox is my favourite,
I like Roblox because it's really fun and exciting,
I am a happy, funny and crazy person,
I am as fast as a cheetah,
My hair is a soft, sandy colour,
My eyes are blue like the sky,
This is me!

Maddy Hewitt (9)
Dringhouses Primary School, York

Welcome To The Amazing World Of Me!

I am a very silly person,
I am a bright flower,
I am a lover of dogs and games, I like dogs because
They're cute and I like games because they're amazing,
I am a fierce and happy person,
I am as strong as a bear,
My hair is as blonde as the sparkly sun,
My eyes are blue like the beautiful sea,
This is me.

Leo March (8)
Dringhouses Primary School, York

This Is Me

You will need;
A joy-filled bedroom
A great big bookshelf
A slab of burgers
The fruit bowl is my best friend
Hundreds of Pokémon cards
An annoying sister too
A pinch of cheekiness
A sprinkle of silliness
800lb of annoyingness
100lb of happiness
1lb of sadness most of the time.

Ted Stenson (7)
Dringhouses Primary School, York

This Is Me

I am great at fighting,
I'm a spy,
I love games, Minecraft is my favourite,
I am a player and want to be a YouTuber,
I am as sneaky as a snake with a cake,
My name can be a kangaroo's,
My eyes are blue like Christopher Escalante's friend Aphmau,
My favourite animal is a penguin.

Joey Butterworth (7)
Dringhouses Primary School, York

Welcome To The Amazing World Of Me!

I am a legendary defender in football,
I am a healthy eater, pizza is my favourite,
I am a lover of cats, Casper the kitten is my favourite because I can tickle his tummy,
I am a clever footballer,
My pets are two fluffy kittens, one huge cat, a lot of fish,
My eyes are faded green,
This is me.

Thomas Swindles (7)
Dringhouses Primary School, York

All About Me

I am a flipper in shiny pink leggings,
I am a cartwheeler spinning across the playground,
I am a lover of nature, flowers are my favourite,
I am a bunny joyful and happy,
I am as kind as my mum and a friend,
My hair is as soft as a cloud,
My eyes are green as a pea pod,
This is me.

Marta Kennedy (7)
Dringhouses Primary School, York

Me And The Future

I am a butterfly in a cocoon,
I am a chocolate bar because I like chocolate,
I am a lover of bunnies, both of my bunnies are my favourite,
I am a graceful bird swooping high,
I am as great as an eagle,
My hair is as gold as the sand,
My eyes are as green as an emerald,
This is me.

Ruby Slater (8)
Dringhouses Primary School, York

The Fascinating Facts About Me

I am a brick wall in football boots,
I am a defender as fast as lightning,
I am a lover of sports, football and cycling are my favourites,
I am a rhino, fearless and strong,
I am a mathematician like a teacher,
My hair is a dark night,
My eyes are as green as grass,
This is me.

Freddie Watson (8)
Dringhouses Primary School, York

Welcome To The Amazing World Of Me!

I am a great gymnast in a rainbow sparkly leotard,
I am a fantastic dancer,
I am a lover of dogs, a black Labrador is my favourite,
I am kind, helpful, and brave,
I am as fast as my kind best friend,
My hair is as brown as chocolate,
My eyes are as blue as the sea,
This is me.

Pixie Freer (7)
Dringhouses Primary School, York

Things About Me

I'm great at sports
I'm great at games
I'm full of fun like an endless flame.
I'm really funny like a comedian.
My favourite food is mouth-watering lobster.
And my favourite colour is blue,
I love nature.
And I'm really good at maths too!
This is me.

Oscar Haslam (9)
Dringhouses Primary School, York

How To Make Me

To make me you will need;
A whole pizza
A silver car
A drop of kindness
A sprinkle of fun.

To create me you will need the following:
Firstly mix gently a drop of kindness.
Next, gently chop and add the pizza.
A sprinkle of fun.
Finally, add a silver car.

Max Kirby (8)
Dringhouses Primary School, York

Who I Am

I am a dog lover,
I am cheeky,
I am a lover of mummy hugs, they are my favourite because they make me feel safe.
I am a good artist and my favourite is drawing.
I am as crazy as a monkey.
My favourite food is cheese pizza.
My eyes are as blue as the sky.
This is me.

Bethany Littler (7)
Dringhouses Primary School, York

The Animal Admirer And The Funny Footballer

I'm an amazing armadillo admirer.
I'm as sneaky as a snake.
I'm as kind as a koala.
I'm as tiny as a tortoise.
But I'm a lightning bolt on the football field.
I'm a superstar striker.
I'm as fast as a powerful Pagani.
This is me!

Roddy Gavin (8)
Dringhouses Primary School, York

My World

I am a tall and messy lion in pyjamas,
I am a fancy but comfy queen,
I am a lover of animals,
Molly is my favourite dog in the whole world,
I am a monkey,
Cheeky and excitable.
My hair is a sheet of silk,
My eyes are blue like the sea,
This is me.

Edie Marchant (8)
Dringhouses Primary School, York

Oxygen Operator

I am Owen, gentle as a field of lavender.
I am as smooth as a slab of pristine rock.
I'm scared as a helpless weak microdot.
I love the character Megatros and,
I love the character Alex, she is a dream.
So now you know more about me.
This is me!

Owen Evans (7)
Dringhouses Primary School, York

Me

I love handwriting,
I love animals,
I love sports,
I am a brilliant basketballer,
I am a tiger,
My favourite pet is an axolotl,
My eyes are like green and a dab of blue,
This is me.

Noah Gibson (7)
Dringhouses Primary School, York

This Is Me

This is me,
I am the imperfect of the perfect,
I am the injustice of the justice,
I am the less of the lesser,
I am the ink on the page,
The scribble,
The mistake,

This is me,
I am the impure of the pure,
I am the inequal of the equal,
I am the minority of the majority,
I am the knot of the string,
I was not meant to be.

No,
This is not me,
I am the unique of the uniqueness,
I am the light in the darkness,
I am the perfect creation of the divine creator,
I was born equal,

I was born free,
I was born me,

I am proud to be a person of colour,
I am who I am,
This is me!

Radiyah Ahmed (9)
Kobi Nazrul Primary School, Whitechapel

This Is Me

I love myself,
I wouldn't change for anyone,
I love my black, silky hair like a mermaid's hair,
I love my dark, brown eyes that are brown as a bear,
I love my pink cheeks that are soft as my fluffy, pink pillow.
I love my red lips that are red as a rose.

I love myself,
I love that I'm kind, caring and loving,
I love that I love to dive into the world of reading,
I love that I'm creative and artistic,
I love that I can skip around in the playground.

I love myself,
I'm beautiful and capable of being the best I can be,
And I love myself, just the way I am.

Khadijah Siddique (7)
Kobi Nazrul Primary School, Whitechapel

This Is My Lifestyle

My name is Yunus,
I love sports,
My favourite sport is football.
I like colouring pictures because of the colours,
I like gaming because it is extremely fun!
I like spicy food and chicken, also noodles,
These are my favourite foods.
My five favourite colours are blue, purple, red, yellow and orange,
My friends are Ismaaeel, Mikael, Adnan, Rafsaan, Chad and Ahian.
My favourite fruits are raspberry, strawberry, blueberry, tangerine, apple, mango, peach, passionfruit, watermelon, pomegranate, pineapple.
My favourite animals are tigers, lions, cheetahs.
My favourite games are Minecraft and Roblox.

Yunus Uddin (7)
Kobi Nazrul Primary School, Whitechapel

Our World

Our world is swirling with green and blue,
From left to right and the middle too.
The sky, the oceans and the trees,
Are all for sight.
The sun is for the morning,
And the moon is for night,
And there are zoos for zebras, giraffes and monkeys,
And farms for cows, horses and donkeys.
There are free animals like fish in herds,
And big and small birds.
There are lots of schools and sheep that make wool.
They are ginormous supermarkets,
And there are swimming pools that make you wet.

Fariha Sayed (10)
Kobi Nazrul Primary School, Whitechapel

Poems To Me!

P oems can bring my life a glimpse of hope,
O ptimistic words wash the way I live like a bar of soap,
E scaping my life to my heart's desire.
M y imagination can bring the fire,
S oul to soul wherever they will go,

T o the hearts of people that I can follow,
O ne word can become a poem to make my heart go fluttery,

M ay you listen to the tune of a sweet, sweet melody
E very single word to my heart sounds heavenly.

Nura Ali (10)
Kobi Nazrul Primary School, Whitechapel

What Me Is

Born in March,
Long and skinny,
They say I was my dad's mini.
London is my town,
Kobi is my school,
BBQ wings make me drool.

Bike rides, Nintendo,
Mad about football,
In the street, the playground, and even in the hall.

Dad loves fried chicken,
Mum needs her tea,
Sister causes trouble and tries to flee!

Some say from Bangladesh,
Others say, "You're British mate!"
I just say, "From flat number eight."

Ismaaeel Choudhury (7)
Kobi Nazrul Primary School, Whitechapel

This Is Me

Black hair, brown eyes,
Not too big or small in size.
This is me!

Sometimes I laugh, sometimes I cry.
I'm always honest, I never lie,
This is me!

I'm a friend and a sister,
I'm also my parents' daughter,
This is me!

I like maths, I like art,
I like some sport to keep a healthy heart,
This is me!

I'm always polite, I'm always kind,
I keep other people's feelings in mind,
This is me!

Ameera Islam (10)
Kobi Nazrul Primary School, Whitechapel

Being Me!

Being me is quite easy.
Being me is fun!
I jump, I skip, I hula hoop.
I also like to run.

Being me is wonderful,
Being me is great!
I have nice clothes,
And when I'm at home,
I eat yummy food from a plate.

Being me is fantastic.
Being me is funny,
I listen to younger children read,
And read them stories to earn some money.

Khadijah Hoque (9)
Kobi Nazrul Primary School, Whitechapel

All About Me

I am playful.
I am cheerful.
I am sometimes shy but I still make friends.
I am creative, I make fun games.
I love everyone around me.
Everyone supports me.
I help people if they are hurt.
I love my toys.
I walk to school.
I sometimes go to the park on my bike.
I tidy up.
I love my whole family.

Amirah Azim (7)
Kobi Nazrul Primary School, Whitechapel

About Myself

I am Iffat.
I can do it all by myself,
I can brush my hair.
I can go anywhere!

About myself,
I can wear my clothes.
I can do everything by myself.
I can do lots of things!

About myself,
I can do some play,
I can do helping,
I can go everywhere!
About myself!

Iffat-Anisha Fazlul Haque Yeasmin (8)
Kobi Nazrul Primary School, Whitechapel

This Is Me

My name is Maisha,
This is me...
A fizzy drink sipper,
A nugget hater,
An animal lover,
A game called wildcraft and other games lover,
This is me...
A light brown skinner,
As brown as tree bark,
A person with hair as dark and brown as chocolate,
And this is me!

Maisha Ali (7)
Kobi Nazrul Primary School, Whitechapel

All About Me

If I were an ingredient
I would be sweetcorn because I am friendly.
My favourite thing about me is swimming because
it helps keep me strong.
My dream for the future is being helpful.
What makes me feel better when I'm sad
Is me cheering other people up.

Sulaiman Ahmed (7)
Kobi Nazrul Primary School, Whitechapel

This Is Me

I am a male, the biggest animal
In the sea is a whale.
Bees make honey,
We make money.
I can make a card,
A tall landmark is the Shard.
My name is Ryan,
I like lions,
I like space,
Shoes have lace.

Ryan Kai (9)
Kobi Nazrul Primary School, Whitechapel

All About Me!

A delicate person with a warming smile,
R ed rosy cheeks as painting as a rose,
S porty person that has a lot of energy,
H elping person with a nice helping hand,
I ndependent is me, Arshi.

Arshi Islam (7)
Kobi Nazrul Primary School, Whitechapel

What Makes Me, Me

I am a boy, I like toys, I like pizza and that's what makes me, me.

I like playing with my friends and making dens,
I like playing with my cousins and siblings too
And that's what makes me, me.

Mikaeel Karim (7)
Kobi Nazrul Primary School, Whitechapel

Me

I'm me
Nobody is just like me,
I'm myself
It's all about me,
A brother, a Muslim
A boy, a shine,
A believer of God, a gamer,
K-pop fan.

Chad Hossin (8)
Kobi Nazrul Primary School, Whitechapel

This Is Me

M y name is Molly and I love my cat, you might not know but she's really fat.
O nly Gracie knows my facts and I also show her Roblox hacks.
L ove my toys and all my friends, our friendship will never end.
L ately, Nibbles has been the star, he was lost in the snow but he didn't go far.
Y es, school is my favourite place but sometimes I have to solve a case.

Molly Fielding
Ponteland Primary School, Ponteland

This Is Me

I'm Takara Barton
I love big and little animals.
I go boarding and I do cool tricks like dolphins.
I also swim in the sea like a playful seahorse.
I always pat the horse's smooth fur like its conditioner and they are big beauties.

Takara Barton (7)
Ponteland Primary School, Ponteland

This Is Me

This is me,
I am a loud young girl with so much to tell you,
But I am quiet when I need to be.
I like Halloween, it's so fun even in my dreams,
If you wait for the time to come you will see.
My favourite season is autumn, is that strange?
I love the warm chilly days that change,
I like dogs, birds and turtles,
I have one dog,
He loves playing around and jumping off logs,
But some winter days he's lazy,
My favourite hobby is to bake, I hope to create a Christmas cake,
I would love to be a police officer
But be successful in football,
I'm still thinking what career should I make?
If I got the opportunity I would take it but should I be something different?
I am British and love fish and chips.
It's so salty on my lips,
This is me, I wouldn't change for the world.

Dolly Griffiths (10)
St Margaret's CE School, Rottingdean

This Is Me

This is me,
This is who I am,
I've nothing I wish to change,
Thank you all,
My mum,
My dad,
For helping me be me,
With my free time in the summer,
I like to play cricket and watch it too,
This is me,
This is who I am,
I've nothing I wish to change,
Whenever I want to draw and paint,
I always have an idea,
A flower in a meadow,
Or maybe a cricket pitch,
Every time I look at myself,
I've nothing I wish to change,
Because... well, this is me.

Isabella Dye (10)
St Margaret's CE School, Rottingdean

This Is Me

I don't want to change, I just won't bother,
I don't think it's right to be one another,
I see no reason not to be me,
Because I am who I want to be,
I'm calm and quiet and choose to obey,
I like that I think it's okay,
I love pets, I have a dog,
I like other animals too,
Like a slimy green frog,
I wish to play football and be a pro,
I could be an artist too, just go with the flow,
Here I am, this is me,
I am who I want to be.

Lily McCaw (10)
St Margaret's CE School, Rottingdean

This Is Me! What I Want To Be

I like art,
I have a go-cart,
I like doodles,
I like poodles,
I like swimming,
I like winning,
I have a dog,
He likes fog,
I have a cat,
Who likes to eat rats,
My dog is called Dennis,
He is such a menace,
My cat is called Brady,
We thought he was a lady,
I think in my head,
What could I be?
My hopes and my dream
Looking at me,

I could be a teacher,
I could be a preacher,
I could be a firefighter,
I could be a paraglider.

Jacob Lord (10)
St Margaret's CE School, Rottingdean

This Is Me

I see my reflection,
And what do I think?
I've got lots of hobbies,
I like pastel pink.

Everyone's different,
And everyone's cool,
I like myself,
Whether short or tall.

Art is a hobby,
And Acro is too,
Climbing on people,
Gymnastics all through.

Like a bluebird,
I get thrown in the air,
Before competitions,
I style my hair.

I like to draw,
As you can see,
In everyday life,
This is me!

Evie Dearnley (10)
St Margaret's CE School, Rottingdean

This Is Me

This is me, I like macaroni,
I have a gecko, and his name is Jeffery,
He lives in my room and he is small,
I love him because he is cool.
I also have a dog, he's lovely and lazy,
But he has five minutes when he's absolutely crazy,
He's only eight weeks, and he loves his treats,
I like to play football,
Although I'm not very tall,
I went to PGL and I found a shell,
I love HP and my name is Albie,
This is me and I'm proud to be me.

Albert Luis Stevenson (10)
St Margaret's CE School, Rottingdean

This Is Me

Football is my sport
Being a sports physio is my dream
Life as a carpenter is a game
I like the hobbit in a Bopit
I depend on my hobbit
Writing stories that are the greatest
Guinea pigs are the cutest
Living at Brighton beach
Hoping to find a teddy bear
Sausages and jam are my bam
Mints, sweets, burgers, ham
Cheese toastie from the villa
Getting my pizza from the geeza
Cakes and chips, Maoams galore,
Living the life of an animator.

Harley Knight (10)
St Margaret's CE School, Rottingdean

This Is Me

A bit about me!
My dreams, goals and who I want to be.
To reach for the stars and be the best I can be
I know if I put my mind to it I will not falter.
My dream job is to be a doctor.
My ambition will never fade away.
I have an amazing family pushing me all the way.
I was born 21st July 2011
My awesome sister is seven
My pets are funny and sometimes cheeky.
I go to the theatre but last time my character was creepy.

Astrid Dickie (10)
St Margaret's CE School, Rottingdean

This Is Me

I look in the mirror,
And what do I see?
Brown hair, blue eyes,
The best I can be,
I love food, especially sweets,
Pizza and pancakes, pasta and meats,
Fish and chips, ketchup and beans,
I am who I am, I will never change me.
I love camping, tent and all,
Although I can't sleep, not good at all,
Campfire and football, rifling aims,
Gaming and reading, fishing and wishing,
I am who I am, this is me.

Albie Knight (10)
St Margaret's CE School, Rottingdean

This Is Me!

This is me!
A dancer I want to be
I want to prance around the stage day and night
This is me!
I love sweets that are sour
And I like to draw flowers
The colours are amazing and
I love the shapes of the petals
This is me!
I think it's cool to listen to R 'n' B
And my favourite hobby is to
Collect crystals near the sea
This is me!
There is no one in the world I want to be.

Danielle Fadario (10)
St Margaret's CE School, Rottingdean

This Is Me

Name is Luke and these are things about me,
I want to be an editor,
Computer tech wreck and smack like you see.
Football, basketball like I see
I like to score and hoop so you see.
I like ping-pong,
Free time is fun 'cause you get to do anything like videos and games.
Favourite food pasta, pizza, like I always eat,
I got one dad, one mum, and obviously one sister and I come from Watford.

Luke Simmons (10)
St Margaret's CE School, Rottingdean

This Is Me

This is me,
When I'm older I want to be a teacher,
I don't want the kids to think I am a preacher.
I don't like clowns,
My smile turns upside down into a frown.
My heart is designed for art but I want to be smart,
I don't want my name to be on the teacher's chart!
I love making, shaking and baking with my annoying sister!
She drives me crazy but I still love her!

Pippa Payne (11)
St Margaret's CE School, Rottingdean

This Is Me

Boxing is my thing,
I like punching inside the ring,
Punching the bag with all my might,
The punching bag puts up a fight,
You're in the ring having a duel,
Sweating a lot trying to keep your cool,
I have an idol called Michael Ali,
They said he danced like a butterfly and stung like a bee,
Punching your opponent as hard as a rock,
Your final punch you get the knock.

Teddy Griffiths (11)
St Margaret's CE School, Rottingdean

This Is Me

I look in the mirror, what do I see?
I see me.
I like lots of sports like football and cricket
I even get lucky to get a ticket.
I like the cream milkshake and pizza.
I have a dream job, a vet and a streetcar racer.
My best friend is Shark who lives near the park
We made a special mark that glows in the dark.
I'm small and great and I have a big spark.
This is me!

Ellison Sedge (11)
St Margaret's CE School, Rottingdean

This Is Me

This is me, I love comedy,
I play a lot of football,
Oh yes really.
I play at the back,
In the shirt number eight.
To make a tackle,
I'm never late.
I love to read,
I love to draw,
And I can even climb,
Up my door!
My dad's a plumber,
I wanna be one too,
Going round people's houses,
And sorting out their loo!

Jack Rowden (10)
St Margaret's CE School, Rottingdean

This Is Me

Hi, I'm Havannah,
My name rhymes with Savannah,
I like to bake
Some yummy cakes,
I have three dogs
Who like to poo logs,
I like poodles
But I prefer doodles,
I used to live
In Milton Keynes,
Now I live in Rottingdean,
I like swimming
And I like winning
I live with my family
I like to have Cadbury.

Havannah Ballard (10)
St Margaret's CE School, Rottingdean

This Is Me

I am ten years old,
I make lip gloss,
That's what I do,
My name is Maya,
When I put it on I turn into a confident girl,
And I love myself even more than drawing, that's me.
I feel as confident as I can be,
I am passionate about it,
So, that's me.

Maya Marco (10)
St Margaret's CE School, Rottingdean

This Is Me

I look in the mirror,
And what do I see?
I see amazing me,
Fish and chips, pasta and cake,
I am a shining star,
Climbing to the very top,
To wanting to be a cop,
Pushing the limits to the sky,
I always have a try,
This is me.

Ying Toong (10)
St Margaret's CE School, Rottingdean

My Story

Hi, my name is Lydia, I'm assuming you want to get to know me.
I like singing, dancing and I love writing stories.
I'm a diabetic and I know it's upsetting but I'm used to it.
But it's a part of me,
And I've learned to embrace it. How?
Well, let me explain.
I have a condition but that doesn't define me!
In fact, it makes me the woman I want to be.
I have such great friends,
You sadly don't know the tall fun girl is such a weirdo!
The ladies who know how to cheer me up at my worst states,
They have good taste in fashion, music, stories and makes great mates.

Lydia Lima Soares Dos Santos (10)
Stanhope Primary School, Greenford

This Is Me!

This is my life,
As an ordinary kid,
Curious and innovative,
I'm not always hid.

Tennis is an engaging sport,
And so is basketball.
But what excites me the most,
Is my passion for volleyball.

I have the kindest family,
Originally from Poland.
I enjoy playing with my cousins
But sadly, I'm in England.

I admire my life in school,
My favourite subject is mathematics.
Maths is my dark horse,
It's just in my genetics.

This is my life,
As an ordinary child.
My future is looking bright,
It's going to be wild.

Franki Raczynski (11)
Stanhope Primary School, Greenford

This Is Me

I consider myself as an ordinary child
Nothing secret, nothing wild
My passion for animals is immense
But the zoos being locked makes me tense.

Me and my siblings originated in the Netherlands
We had to be moved to England
Family and cousins being locked in my heart
I set my goals on a dart.

My future desire is to be a doctor
However, it would be nice to be in a tractor
Helping people would be a goal
Only with a light-hearted soul.

Anoja Nadarasa (11)
Stanhope Primary School, Greenford

All My Life

I love football,
I always have to shoot the ball,
I love being a striker,
I am a striker fighter,
I love Neymar, Mbappe, Ronaldo, Messi and more,
But did you know my favourite number is four?
I love drawing,
You may think it's boring,
I love ice cream it makes me feel nice,
But one thing for sure is that I don't like rice,
Everybody knows that rice is not nice!
This is me,
My favourite movies are Despicable Me 1, 2 and 3.

Amina Baahmed (8)
Stanhope Primary School, Greenford

This Is Me

I am the star that shines bright
With extreme light
In the ravishing night.

I am the flower that blooms
Whilst taking energy from the moon
And I shiver when the night is full of gloom.

I loom over
A green clover
As my lucky life
Is filled with good luck.

I am me that acts
Like a moon
In the gloomy room.

This is my beautiful life
My future is looking
Immensely bright
This is me.

Dunmolaoluwa Hannah Ojo (10)
Stanhope Primary School, Greenford

This Is Me

T onight I am going to munch through my favourite food, peri-peri chicken
H owever I prefer to eat my mum's biryani
I like to play basketball with my friends
S ometimes I like to dance.

I read Jacqueline Wilson books
S uddenly, I'll go to my favourite cousin's house and play with them.

M y favourite time of day is when going to bed to snooze
E very day I am myself.

Shruthi Sellathamby (10)
Stanhope Primary School, Greenford

Kaiden

T his is what I do every day
H is ball gets stolen all the time
I ntelligent is my thing
S easide has a king crab.

I like everything
S o I can do what I want.

K icking the tree 'cause I'm mad
A bird killer in my house
I like football
D en in the garden
E xcellent at maths
N ot ten I'm eight.

Kaiden Watson (8)
Stanhope Primary School, Greenford

This Is Me

T he game that I like to play is Fortnite.
H eavy rain is my favourite because I can jump in puddles.
I like racing games because I can drive fast cars.
S cary rides are my favourite at the beach.

I like playing football with the year 4s.
S nakes are my favourite reptile.

M inecraft is a funny game.
E very day I play Roblox and Pokémon Go.

Anwar Dardak (7)
Stanhope Primary School, Greenford

This Is Me

T aking care of people.
H elping people out.
I have a pen license.
S ometimes I like to play golf.

I am eight years old.
S ometimes I go to the shop.

A raani is my name.
R ainbow is my favourite thing.
A lso, I go to school.
A lways, I am confident.
N ever give up like me.
I am good at maths.

Araani Sivasubramaniam (8)
Stanhope Primary School, Greenford

All About Me

I am creative
I am bright
And to everyone I meet
I'm a delight!

I am mainly energetic, vibrant and magnetic
Just like a crowd
But sometimes my friends say I'm a bit too loud.

Singing and writing are my passion
I will and always have had a good sense of fashion
I hope you have learnt a lot about me, a poem session,
But be careful... I might scare you like a bee.

Charlize Erese (11)
Stanhope Primary School, Greenford

This Is Harper

T he best dancer
H appy where I live
I s the happiest in the world.
S o I like ice cream.

I live in a house
S o happy when I do English.

H ave the best pets.
A good runner.
R epresent science fair.
P eople I like.
E asy maths I like
R eally happy when I eat my favourite food.

Harper Nolan (8)
Stanhope Primary School, Greenford

About Me

I am a boy,
People call me
Sean, I like
The warm house,
It calms my
Mind, I love to
Play football,
I strike the ball
On the pitch, my
Shrine.

My favourite colour
Is red and white
Representing England
In all its might,
I am intelligent,
Chaotic, and
One to laugh.

This is my
Life, my future
Is looking bright!

Sean Butt (10)
Stanhope Primary School, Greenford

Colours Of The Rainbow

When I close my eyes,
I see millions of colours like explosive fireworks creating even more colours.
I think they are dream eggs waiting to hatch.
Line, shape and colour are elements of art.
Texture, space and value that's where I start.
When I use what I know as an artist, I will grow.
Line, shape, colour, texture, space and value...
The ABCs of art.

Sana Hashimi (10)
Stanhope Primary School, Greenford

All About Me

T hings that I own are fun
H ave very fun games that you can play
I really love my furry dog
S easides are my favourite place to play.

I like to play on my PS4
S ometimes I play too much!

M e and my friends like to play football
E lephants are my favourite animal because they can spit water.

Dipanshu Shah (7)
Stanhope Primary School, Greenford

Zara's Poem

T hursday is my favourite day
H appiness is skating in the ice rink
I have so many lovely friends
S wimming is my favourite sport to do.

I like my family
S ometimes I like to go to the cinema and go to the park.

M y birthday is on March 19th
E very day I try to work hard and hard.

Zara Hussein (7)
Stanhope Primary School, Greenford

This Is Me, Armin

T he favourite cartoon I like is Alvin and the Chipmunks
H arry Potter is my favourite movie
I ce cream is my favourite dessert
S miggle is my favourite shop.

I love Milky Way bars
S miling like sunshine.

M y favourite device is a Chromebook
E very day I watch something.

Armin Saberipour (7)
Stanhope Primary School, Greenford

This Is Me

The hard work I crave is a mystery,
A remarkable fast mind,
Confident with a humble heart,
That's right.

My face shines with diversity,
I am sweet and sometimes sour depending on the hour,
Close to my heart is friends but closest is family,

My goals are my drive which I strive towards happily,
This is me.

Dorcas Nsubuga (11)
Stanhope Primary School, Greenford

This Is Me

I like winter even though I was born in the summer.
My mamma does the best pizza.
My favourite animal is a pelican because it's delicate.
My favourite TV show is Grizzly and the Lemmings which makes me forget my life.
I like playing Spider-Man with my friend Jayden.
I like mango because it's as sweet as sugar.
This is me.

Marwan Sidani (10)
Stanhope Primary School, Greenford

All About Me

T oyshops are my favourite places.
H ave lots of caring friends.
I love my family.
S tanhope is a very caring school.

I t's always a good day.
S easides are always cold every day.

M y family cares so much about me.
E ating is one of my favourite hobbies.

Camiyah Tuahene Richards (7)
Stanhope Primary School, Greenford

All About Me, Tnishpreet Kaur

T he colour blue is my favourite
H ave many toys that I might get
I love getting new toys
S ometimes I am naughty.

I love swimming and karate class
S lides are very fun!

M e and my friends love swimming
E very day after school my friends come to play.

Tnishpreet Kaur (7)
Stanhope Primary School, Greenford

This Is Riaz

R espectful and kind, it's all in my name.
I ce or rice that's quite nice, but I won't eat anything like mice.
A nnoying? I can be, but not all the time, that's just not me.
Z ... that's a hard one. What can I say? I love my bed, there I can sleep the night away. *Zzzzz.*

Riaz Mahabir (11)
Stanhope Primary School, Greenford

Anmol's Poem

T all in size
H ave quiet fish at home
I like to play on my PS4
S oap is my favourite thing to wash my hands with.

I play Rocket League on my Xbox
S ome video games can always cheer me up.

M y family is the best
E ating pizza is the best!

Anmol Singh (7)
Stanhope Primary School, Greenford

This Is Me

T all in size
H ave an annoying brother
I love playing Rocket League
S ometimes I play on my dad's PS4.

I really like chocolate
S ometimes I eat sweets.

M e and Kaiden like to joke around
E lephants are my favourite animals.

Corey Watson (7)
Stanhope Primary School, Greenford

This Is Me

I am the light
That shines bright
In the night.

My favourite colour is green
I like to eat peas
Little do I know
I am just being me.

I am sugar and spice
With a little bit of nice
I am hard to find.

I am a flower
That blooms
In the gloomy noon.

Sana Usman (10)
Stanhope Primary School, Greenford

Singing Time

S inging is the best,
I love it,
N o shouting here,
G o break the record!
I won the competition,
N ow I'm glad,
G o and chill out!

T oo cool,
I love to sing,
M e and you,
E xercise!

Nesha Angelova (9)
Stanhope Primary School, Greenford

This Is Me

T he colour purple is my favourite colour.
H aving a party for my birthday.
I like art.
S chool is fun!

I love puppies.
S cience is my favourite subject.

M e and my friends like movies.
E lephants are cool.

Ellia Demiri (8)
Stanhope Primary School, Greenford

Zayan's Poem All About Me

T uesday is my favourite day
H ave a sister
I have lots of nice friends
S even is my age.

I like to play games
S easide is my favourite place.

M y TV is huge
E very day I try hard and never give up.

Zayan Hamid (7)
Stanhope Primary School, Greenford

I Am Who I Am

I am a bird tweeting.
I am a lion eating.
I am a tree dancing.
I am a runner prancing.
I am Spider-Man climbing.
I am a Sonic creator.
I am a math problem solver.
I am a Chelsea fan.
I am in a rocking band.
I am who I am.

Gulled Talyanle (11)
Stanhope Primary School, Greenford

This Is Me

This is me...
I am eight years old.
I love dog puppies.
I have a brother.
Who is a lover.

I love going out.
My hobby is art.
I love going shopping.
I love my teacher.
My teacher is Mrs Sead.

Shalini Aruchuna (8)
Stanhope Primary School, Greenford

Odai

O rdinarily I'm the best at football
D inosaurs are not scary to me
A bsolutely I like creatures
I have diamond sisters.

Odai Alarabi (7)
Stanhope Primary School, Greenford

Zain

Z ain loves a zebra
A mazing at PE
I love chocolate chip ice cream
N ature is a victorious thing.

Zain Adeen (7)
Stanhope Primary School, Greenford

Sofia

S oft brown curly hair
O wn a nine-year-old cat
F riendly
I ntelligent
A cat lover.

Sofia Wozniak (7)
Stanhope Primary School, Greenford

YOUNG WRITERS INFORMATION

We hope you have enjoyed reading this book – and that you will continue to in the coming years.

If you're the parent or family member of an enthusiastic poet or story writer, do visit our website **www.youngwriters.co.uk/subscribe** and sign up to receive news, competitions, writing challenges and tips, activities and much, much more! There's lots to keep budding writers motivated!

If you would like to order further copies of this book, or any of our other titles, then please give us a call or order via your online account.

Young Writers
Remus House
Coltsfoot Drive
Peterborough
PE2 9BF
(01733) 890066
info@youngwriters.co.uk

Join in the conversation!
Tips, news, giveaways and much more!

YoungWritersUK **YoungWritersCW** **youngwriterscw**